MAGNUM MYSTERIUM

Born in Chicago in 1954, **Julie O'Callaghan** has lived in Ireland since 1974. Her collections of poetry include *Edible Anecdotes* (Dolmen Press, 1983), a Poetry Book Society Recommendation; *What's What* (Bloodaxe Books, 1991), a Poetry Book Society Choice; *No Can Do* (Bloodaxe Books, 2000), a Poetry Book Society Recommendation; *Tell Me This Is Normal: New & Selected Poems* (Bloodaxe Books, 2008), a Poetry Book Society Recommendation; and *Magnum Mysterium* (Bloodaxe Books, 2020). Her books of poetry for older children include *Taking My Pen for a Walk* (Orchard Books, 1988), *Two Barks* (Bloodaxe Books, 1998) and *The Book of Whispers* (Faber & Faber, 2006). She has received the Michael Hartnett Award for poetry and is a member of the Irish academy of arts, Aosdána.

JULIE O'CALLAGHAN

Magnum
Mysterium

BLOODAXE BOOKS

First published 2020 by
Bloodaxe Books Ltd,
Eastburn,
South Park,
Hexham,
Northumberland NE46 1BS,

www.bloodaxebooks.com
For further information about Bloodaxe titles
please visit our website and join our mailing list
or write to the above address for a catalogue

Supported using public funding by
ARTS COUNCIL
ENGLAND

Cover design: Neil Astley & Pamela Robertson-Pearce.

Printed in Great Britain by Bell & Bain Limited, Glasgow, Scotland, on
acid-free paper sourced from mills with FSC chain of custody certification.

For Dennis

ACKNOWLEDGEMENTS

Some of these poems were previously published in: *The Irish Times*, *The Moth*, *The New Statesman*, *Poetry Ireland Review*, *Stony Thursday Book*, and *The Times Literary Supplement*.

Thanks to the Irish Arts Council and Aosdána – the Irish academy of arts – for their generous support during the writing of these poems.

CONTENTS

AFTER DENNIS O'DRISCOLL

Island Life

I live on an island.
But that's not the worst part.
Water sloshes uncontrollably
at the edges
of this entire geological formation.
You can hardly
go anyplace
without falling off.

Sitting in a Cloud

The Irish monk
in his igloo of stone
inhabits a rock
jutting up from the ocean.
Sitting in a cloud
he watches weather approaching.
Where does it come from?
Beyond the known universe.
Beyond the realm of knowledge.
From a direction never mapped.

Voyage

This guy Magellan,
looking for the Spice Islands:
he's on a huge sailboat
and he pretty much
hasn't got the foggiest idea
what he's doing.
For instance
what happens if he's sailing along
and the ocean just ends
and he falls off the planet?
He doesn't know how far
the water extends.
He'd really like the data on what's
beyond the H_2O
(or even IF there is a beyond).
He keeps telling himself
to stay calm
it will all work out
– those blasted Spice Islands will appear
any second
just over the horizon.
Absolutely.

After Gulliver

Little Green Fields by Gerard Dillon

Cast forlornly upon the whaleish waters,
flailing about,
by some miracle, land appeared.
Thereafter I swam with hope
extending my legs downward
searching for the sandy floor
I knew must lie below.

My foot landed softly:
I would live more.

Crawling monster-wise
onto a small beach,
burrowing to sleep
under the blanket of sand crystals
my new home provided
until sun tapped my cheek.
Whereupon I gazed crustily
in all directions
discovering what place this was
I had pioneered.
First vision:
Little Green Fields.

Second vision:
how little green fields
are sometimes blue and pink
and over in that direction are orange.
Each a kingdom,
each a stone-barricaded world.
The Realm of the Chicken,

District of Tillage, White Cottage Province,
Horse-scratching Region,
The Universe for Leaning and Smoking
Beside a Buried Saint
Lying in the soil beneath your feet
and the Zone for Ancient Structures
here and there telling old stories
to which no one is listening.

Third sight:
there is only one gateway
through these little green fields.
I have searched everywhere
and found this tiny wooden
barrier on hinges.
It leads to the mysterious
green field yard
of stone wonder.

Here is where I carved my name.

MAXIMUM CAR WASH

It might be exactly like
this conveyor-belt car wash.
The notices are the same:
PUT CAR IN NEUTRAL.
HANDBRAKE OFF.
DO NOT STEER.
You let go
– sit back –
and even though
it grows dark
you allow the suds
and the sprayers
to obliterate the world.
You travel along
(somewhere – nowhere)
so quietly and lightly
that you know
everything will be OK.
Giant whirring brushes
gently nudge you
as you journey.
Brilliant light ahead:
a new start.

Zen Christmas

To be Zen
facing into Christmas.
As if, in a canoe,
you suddenly hear
thundering rapids
around the next
bend in the river,
and become
very calm
very strong
very stoic.

Now open your eyes.
It's St Stephen's Day.
You are still alive.
Your canoe has not
crashed on a rock.
What's more
you are holding
a big hunk
of juicy leftover turkey
on your fork.

Norman Rockwell's Apples

The usual bureaucracy
with American nature:
signs scolding us
not to even think
about eating these apples.
What is this?
The garden of Eden?

Maybe it is.
We sit on a bench
eyeing the Housatonic River Valley
enviously in the fall heat.
Norman Rockwell's apples
hidden away
in our pockets.

Riddle

Christ's tongue   clang
blasts battle   clatter
calls the warning   da-dong
ring of danger   da-ding

sings a wedding   cling
prays vespers   blang
cries holy blessings   blong
chants of sorrow – a soul gone   gong

No Longer with Us

Dropping my tea bag
into the compost garbage
I look up –
here's a row of old-timers
swinging their legs
off the top of our stone wall.
It's a great Kildare day
so they figured
they'd catch a few rays.
I glance over at them
(I don't want to
make them self-conscious)
and execute a
'howdy neighbour' wave.
People who are no longer
with us deserve
an Irish spring day, too,
– right?
When I am no longer
with us
I will sit on that wall
doing the same.

Horse Power

The horses are waiting.
They look over
stable doors patiently.
They know what's ahead
and they forgive us
our hundred years
of neglect.
They are building up
their strength with
oats and grass and hay,
getting ready for their comeback.
You can put your foot
down on the accelerator
all you want –
overtake, honk, tailgate:
the horses sense
what's happening
deep under their feet.

The Day

When the day came
(oh it comes)
and the big old horse
is too stiff
to be ridden
his owner
carries a little chair
into his stable
and reads him poetry
instead.

Floating World

Hot night
floating
turquoise pool

skyscraper roof
black sky
floats over me

dreams float
like stars
like fireflies

oh you
are there
I can see you

from where
I lie in the pool
up in the sky

Headlights

stuck in traffic
gazing at the sky
trying not to dwell
on the bad thing
that happened
I try with all my might
inching forward
before sunrise
the car, the radio
the heat – hit the
window button
and keep trying to stop
that bad thing
from my thoughts

out of a dark cloud
the headlights of a plane
blaze across the sky
and I whisper
oh that's where you went

The Bridge-Tender I Didn't Call Dad

In the box labelled FATHER'S OCCUPATION
on my birth certificate
it says 'Bridge-Tender'.

He saved a few people
who jumped into the
Chicago River.

But mostly he raised
the bridge
if a tall boat

needed to get through.
We visited him once
over at the Michigan Avenue Bridge.

The Bridge Tower
was rather dingy
– he read a lot.

He tended bridges
when I was born.
I called him Jack.

News

The postcard has just arrived
announcing that I've been born.
It took 50 years to arrive.
The two cent stamp
might have something to do with that.
I flip the card over
and there I am howling
in my mom's
flowery lap.
It's written
in that upbeat Jesuit handwriting
Jack specialised in.
Well I'm still here,
still cranky.

Beside Me

In the lobby
I am perspiring under
layers of winter-woollens
and memories.
Snow cascades outside
And sleds are sliding
inside my head.
I watch the elevator numbers
descending from floor 22
and when the doors open
and no one gets out
I know you're sprawling
on the fake-leather lobby chair
beside me.

Unfunny

Some things are funny.
But not this.
There isn't even one
humorous aspect
about you getting cancer
and dying.
Believe me –
I've thought about it
from all angles.
You should be here
for the new millennium
not scattered
in Lake Michigan.

Last 4th

(Jack)

I looked over at you
gazing out across the city
with fireworks on the horizon
from your bedroom window
and knew.
No more holiday picnic lunches
in the park for you.
Then I heard you thinking:
this is my last 4th
I will never watch fireworks again.
The rest of us pointed to the zingers
exploding in the distance.

Stay

You and I, Jack,
seated on a most comfortable rock.
The sun blasts everything
in this scene.
Who can make me laugh
like you could?
A commodious rock
located in Connemara
years ago.
You sure did annoy me
sometimes.
We're chewing the fat
on a couch-like rock
in the wilds of Galway
facing the direction of the new world.
Just think of all our ancestors
jumping off this island
headed west.
You get up off this rock
and fly away.
I get up off this rock
and stay.

Ship

I didn't forget you.
You are the one
not in Chicago
where you ought to be.
You're the person
who should be biking
along the lake shore
observing migrating birds.
When I heard
oh build your ship of death, oh build it!
I obviously
thought how lucky you were –
sailing was so your THING.
But still –
I worry about
the sufficiency
of your accoutrements
out in the sea of
eternal life.

Garden Daydream

orange poppies
no one can see me
cosmos – pink and white
I am dreaming
dark leaf dahlia
it is September
blue delphiniums
I have things to do
daisies
winter is coming
scented sweetpea
I won't forget you
bell flower
go to sleep
pale hollyhock
who will I be
climbing rose
I smell you
gravel pathway
what is simple
green foliage
frost will sparkle
small crimson flower
I will look for you
next year
dream garden –
everyone
leave me alone

Bruisers with Groceries

give me hope.
They're normally heading out
to a night of beer cans,
onion dip, cheezeroos and hula-hoops.

But a while ago they gazed around
their shabby room
and remembered actual meals.
Hot and with gravy.

The bruisers mosey down
to the store – trying to remember
what normal people eat.
There is a limit to tater-tots.

Ice Age

During my ice age
icicles were a major factor –
forming on roof gutters
and tree branches,
they were the earliest known
version of the light sabre.

We found we could
bake ice into shapes
such as an ice rink
with floodlights and cheesy music
down at the beach
beside the frozen waves.

And it was during my ice age
that a storm encased
the world in a layer of crystal.
We chipped away at it
like baby birds
pecking out of a translucent egg.

Seasonal Affective Disorder

It starts in September.
You can sense it
in your bones.
Some, panic and sweat
imagining the months ahead
in dreary detail.
Then deeper into the abyss.
But, on the shortest day,
I discover
a golden thread
of light
illuminating the chamber
of our hallway
through the spyhole.
My ancient DNA
instructs me
to worship the sun.

Distant Memory

Summer is the season
I can hardly recall
it seems so distant.
I can't remember
my feet either
they are so covered up
under three layers of socks.
They used to be
nicely tanned, I think,
with beaded flip-flops
of some description
down there
I can vaguely imagine.
Feet, hang in there.
And Me – under sweaters,
cardigans, t-shirts, blankets, duvets
(I know I'm under here somewhere)
– you hang in there too.

New Year's Omens

If the wind is from the west
on New Year's Eve,
our island will flourish.
And the first foot to enter
our dwelling on New Year's Day
should be the boot
of a black-haired man or boy.
Let's not forget the cake theory
and how we all need to throw
barmbrack at our front doors
to banish hunger and famine.
A time of bells, fires,
the banging of pots
and omens for the coming year.
Some say that dropping a plate
on the first day
guarantees a special year.
That's why I will be
eating the cake
– not throwing it –
and dropping the plate
for a cracking good year.

Hidden

I need to find something...
Not behind the gates
of Ed Rusky Ford dealership.
Let's skip Moody's Pub and Grill.
It is so hidden.
My father
showed me how to find it
many years ago.
I pass Dollar Discount,
Afro-Hair Extensions,
Glamor Girl, 2nd Time Round
Pre-owned Clothes and Accessories
and Chucky's Chuck House Steaks.
Plastic palm trees
across the street at White Castle.

I place my eye
at the gap in a wooden garage door
and there it is:
the 12 foot high
Golden Seated Buddha
I was seeking.

*

The apartment she lived in
with her dad
was near Lincoln Park.

Furniture had been
abandoned in favour of
tree ferns, banana fronds,
branches, leaves, trunks.

Pushing aside Amazonian décor
we hiked deep into
rainforest looking for a clearing.

Our machetes cleared a path
to the outside world
with Chicago Blizzard.

*

In the heat
with your relatives.
Signs
saying do this don't do that.
Meandering sweating
upright mammals
in sports shoes and shorts.

Zoom into the canyon
– the cliff face opposite
below your feet an adobe vision
an ancient city
with windows ladders
doorways nestled on a ledge.

*

Pre-history:
a rainy Irish day
staring out
a museum window
watching drops
on glass
wishing it would cease
– something miraculous –
crouching out in the rain

on the opposite window ledge:
a tiny ancient adobe village
with windows ladders
doorways nestled into red brick.

*

it is usually hidden
you feel it sometimes
but then
you tell yourself:
knock it off

it is hidden
it gives you a twinge
or a punch
deep – somewhere
you don't want to go

21st Century Pillow Book

IN TRAFFIC

Three things
which should never be seen
in traffic:
phone at ear
obscene finger gesture
speeding teenager

PARKING LOTS

Here is a tricky subject
why do people
open doors and scratch my car
lift babies and scratch my car
push grocery trolleys and scratch my car
you are considered cranky
if you mention it
but it really is highly annoying

THE OFFICE

Three conundrums:
collection for person you can't stand
overhearing colleagues talking about you
doing what the new boss says

FASHION TRENDS

Yes yes – I am not a young person
so call me an old biddy if you want
but this wearing of tight little tops
with midriffs on view – idiotic.
Blubber is not a gorgeous sight
is it?
And teaming that with low tight jeans
only makes it worse.
Even if the blub is minimal
the waistbands are so snug
that any flesh at all bunches up
and hangs over
in almost every case.
We don't wish to see this.
When future generations
see photos of you,
you will thank me
for my advice.

PLASTIC SURGERY

No one wants to get old anymore.
You might see a woman
with a glowing dewy complexion
not a wrinkle or line or sag
and envy her beauty.
Then several days later
you hear she has had a facelift.
How confusing.

SKYSCRAPERS

Nothing can be more deeply moving
than standing on the roof
of a 30-storey building
beside a shimmering pool
of turquoise water
and gazing down out at the city
in all directions.
If it is a balmy summer night
and stars are overhead
and lights from other buildings
are glowing in the distance
I am overcome
with happiness
with sadness.

CHILDREN

Why do parents these days
pamper and spoil their offspring?
I will never understand it.
Gucci baby booties, Dior romper suits,
tiny tots math classes and personal trainers
and mini computer programs.
A four year old is driven to
his Mozart appreciation class
and warns his mother
to be sure to pick him up on time.
He doesn't want to miss
his favorite cartoon.
Has the world gone crazy?

THINGS THAT FALL FROM THE SKY

Dying embers from fireworks,
box kites on a still day,
faulty satellites
badly serviced airplanes,
acid rain,
ducks shot in the chest,
flying saucers

ONCE WHEN I VISITED THE MALL

I bought a magnificent floral skirt
the one I had been searching for
which I knew would be perfect
for every occasion.
But at home
the flowers seemed faded.

THINGS WITHOUT MERIT

Reality TV shows,
nuclear waste,
OTT bling,
Hollywood actors giving interviews,
pop stars giving interviews
sub-standard organic produce

Departure Drama

Another sorrowful scene
unfolds
under the Drake Hotel palms
amidst the tea cups
– to a harp accompaniment.
How can we possibly
enact this drama again?
We are familiar
with our lines.
It gets more gnarly
with each performance.
Daughter – flying home to Ireland.
Mother – boards bus down Lake Shore Drive
to Sheridan Road.

The airport coach is late.
I wish I could skip this vision
of you walking toward
the setting sun
to Michigan Avenue
like a little girl
with a toy in a bag.

Mother in a Twister

Light
from under her door
illuminates my foot.
Deep night
high in the apartment.

Ear to wood
I hear
the ferocious
tornado roar on
the other side.

A gust blasts
my ankles.
Her rosary sways
on the handle.
Is she asleep?

I imagine
she must be swirling
around the room on her bed.
I'm paralysed.
What to do?

Broken

Something gets broken
that will never be repaired.
No use trying to fix it.
Not possible.
Once it's banjaxed
you just have to
live with it.
Join the club.
Everybody is looking for
maximum strength
mega-hold superglue.

Call

Now time
for summoning
my ancients.
Try it.
Broadcast
to all sectors
worm holes
and other universes.
Although your ancestors roam
the Happy Hunting Grounds
they appreciate a little attention
or a thought for all that
DNA they handed down to you.

Early on Indian Hill

It is very early
on Indian Hill
but she is outside
in her pjs rearranging
surprisingly colourful
tiny ceramic figurines
under the succulents
with a backdrop
of sunshine burning
the mist in the valley.
Sometimes she shades her eyes
and stands watching her
pet bluebird sipping
at the pottery water-holder.
But only for a short time
because the lavender
needs to be dealt with
and the garden
requires a particular arch
of water sprayed on it.
And anyway
she doesn't want
the iridescent
hummingbirds to feel
under-appreciated.
Busy busy
early on Indian Hill.

Teensy Tomatoes

Long ago
I'd wake up
with stinky tomato leaves
touching my face
out on the porch
overlooking Lake Michigan
where I spent nights
pretending to sleep.
The sun tended to rise
from the water
(wakey-wakey)
permeating my forehead
with rays.
I pushed aside
various branches
to view the vista
from a cheek-on-pillow
perspective.
The lake lounged sideways
in artistic
shadings and reflectings
in a most pre-historic way.
We plucked teensy tinsy tomatoes
and with a super-sharp implement
divided them up between us
and ate them as if our lives
depended on it.

Perfect World

How convenient
that most of us
have heads
which fit in
under the stratosphere.
And the way pebbles
are the exact right size
for a human hand.
When trying to
free up a rock
from my flower-bed
I have faith
that what looms
in the underworld of mud
is not the size
of a juggernaut.
Crossable rivers,
trees shading us –
how oceans are a challenge
(in a good way!)
Vegetables delivering
the perfect nutrients
for ungrateful old us.
Strawberries
exactly corresponding
to pie holes.
Why so?
To what do we owe
these honours?
Canines evolving
into seeing-eye dogs
just to stop us
tripping on a curb.

Festivities

It doesn't do me a bit of good
seeing the lake like this:
bleak – frozen – uninviting.
But mumsy in her festive mode
is grinding those early morning
blasted coffee beans
nuking my ears with churning
screeching, nasty noise
(oh I know – I'll miss that sound
in years to come).
But just at the moment I'm wondering
if you're dancing out there in the blizzard?
I can see right into it
and maybe that's you over there
swooping around?
We're all lined up on the couch
under your fake Georgia O'Keeffe cloud painting
We are being extremely US.
WFMT/coffee grinding/picture sitting
inside a blizzard – so cosy you could almost
spread your wings and
show us the new you.

Purchasing Vittles

Foraging for Christmas dinner
members of my clan and I
graze the cake department
sample the party dip
nibble the exotic fruit segments
negotiating minor
aisle squirmishes
with our grocery carts
at Whole Foods, Christmas Eve.
Ho-ho-ho – a foreign gentleman
is polishing the celery display.
An artiste is assembling
an Arcimboldo
of vegetable matter.
How very very.
A flowing ribbon receipt
will tie up our holiday.

At Whole Foods

Entering shangri-la
pushing a dinky deep-green cart
fragrant fruit and flowers flavour the air.

But then – Wham! Conflict Alert!
Gal in baseball cap and Whole Foods apron
raising voice at 12 o'clock.

Trouble in Paradise:
'You thought I didn't hear you.
But I heard you.

You were making fun of me
behind my back.
Oh I heard you.

That doesn't fly with me.'
The easy part here is arranging the produce
into shiny tableaux of loveliness.

Nuclear Bombs

I disremembered how I've got resources
in the bank of heavenly credits!
Nuclear bomb drill in 1962:
I recited 3 gajillion of those
mini-prayers covering my head:
Jesus, Mary and Joseph
crouching on the stairway
of St Ignatius
with my fellow-scholars
and thinking *you have got to be kidding me.*
OK. So now I get to go straight
to Heaven.
Ker-ching!

A Cabin in the Berkshires

VOICES

I hear
people's voices
out in the forest
with the crickets
– then I remember
the babbling brook

ME IN IT

rolling thunder
in the forest hills
tree house in foliage
highlighted by moonbeam
stream
insect noises
carved leather notebook
lightning
racoon hiding
tree house
and me in it

STORM

crashing rain
bashing the tree house roof
if it comes through the screens
I'll wait to see the moon
shine on the forest
bears are waiting somewhere
for the sound of
a stick with bells

TRAIN MUSIC

this is what
I was trying to remember:
sad train moan
in the heat
howling
to the nation

CRICKETS

crash-landing
into a cabin in a forest
sit and look
at the Mr Coffee coffee-maker
wooden beams
colourful bells
on the bear stick
all well and good
– to the crickets
I would like to suggest:
COULD WE GIVE IT A REST?

FOREST LIFE

I live in a forest
but that's not
the best part
gradations of green leaves
shake uncontrollably
up and down
this entire botanical formation.
You can hardly stand anywhere
without falling into a dream.

WHAT?

How can this be October
if I'm sitting
amidst tree branches
sweating
with no shoes on

LAST DAY

My last day
of forest adventures
has it all:
quiet in every direction.
A poem
of autumn heat
with stream
murmuring.

United Nations

The earth is so tiny
that I'm on the 147 Lake Shore Drive Express
beside a Russian lady
with red hair and dagger nails
who seems at home in Chicago.
The cranky geezer
across the aisle
is like an old pioneer
from the Rockies
who growls at the Tibetan young folk
with FREE TIBET posters to
watch it with those posters
they could hurt somebody.
The Guatemalan mother
tells her daughter to sit still.
A huge Chicagoan
holds an enormous transistor radio
up to his ear and commences talking
into it – pretending it's his cellphone.
This country used to be my home.

Peaceful Valley

I dock
my unidentified flying forehead
into the tranquil tweed valley
of your shoulder blades
transferring data
of peace
from this region
directly into my
hard drive.

Check the Fridge

At a certain stage
I yawn to myself,
'haul yourself up
out of the scratcher, my friend,
for another challenging day
of human interaction.'
I extract myself
in the approved manner:
roll on side
place left foot on floor
place right foot on floor.
Upright – I notice
a strange listing to the proceedings.
Earthquake?
I open the curtains
and note how me and my house
are at sea, floating.
No land in site.
I climb back into bed
and think.
No phone reception out here.
We'll be in California
in a couple of years.
I go and check the fridge.

Mystery

I was saying to the little girl
how we'd better not bother
her neighbour.

She was getting ready
for her baby to arrive.

'But *how* do you get ready?'

I mention a crib
and toys and clothes for the baby.

Scrunching her face,
'You mean it comes *NAKED* –
without even a towel around it?'

Babu will show you to your room

we follow Babu
    he turns
        we turn

he enters a corridor
    with us behind
        he trots down stairs
            we do the same

more turns
    further hallways
        through a lounge
            veering left
                around a corner

we wonder
    how far more
        Babu can
            lead us

is it possible
    this journey
        is never-ending?

we do not ask
    we are Babu's followers:
        holding hands

since that's what
    Hansel and Gretel do
        when they get nervous

AFTER DENNIS O'DRISCOLL

Magnum Mysterium

BEYOND

Oh Dennis, I dream of you
in the northwest provinces
beyond communication
with the known world.
Who do you speak with?
In what language?
I'm sure you forget all about us
here in the ocean
surrounded by sea monsters.
I eat bowls of food
alone at the table
wondering where you are
my husband.

SOLITARY CONFINEMENT

The rattling keys
in my hand
I come
to our front door
enter
and
lock myself in
set the alarm
and commence
my Life Sentence.

PREDICTION

The Mayans
foretold
the end of the world
for December 21st 2012.
Credit where it's due:
They weren't far off.

The end of OUR world:
December 24th 2012.

NUCLEAR BOMBS 2

The nuns
taught us
to sit on the stairs
and cover our heads
in the event
of a communist
bomb attack
reciting Holy Phrases.
I sit on the stairs
I cover my head
and say over and over
– you will
never
come
back.

CAN I BE HONEST WITH YOU?

I'm not doing all that well.
I bow my head –
there is nothing I can see.
I can not look
at these rooms you lived in
I can't look
at the chair you sat in
(your tweed jacket where you left it)
– what use would that be?
I bow my head
in this town we lived in
on this road you walked on
What is possible?
Not this.
I can't look anywhere.

FORMATIONS

Den, there go those
damn birds
squawking and flapping
above us all
like they always do in spring and autumn
in those hatefully beautiful formations.
Vs flying somewhere
over yonder.
I'm crying for you
at my desk in Trinity
watching this horrible
magnificent rotten sight
I can't tell you about.

SEMPERVIVUM

living forever??
not tempting at all
I guess you know all the secrets
of the universe
by now
you sure wondered for long enough
I planted sempervivums
on your grave

THE GENIUS OF THE UNIVERSE:

meat + vegetables
feet + socks
me + you
try explaining that
on a blackboard of
doodles a mile long
in MIT – you'd never
figure it out
oh god

MEDIUM

you say it's Wednesday night
put out the recycling garbage cans this week
I hear that loud and clear
you say get to work on your poems
you say stop wasting time
do some vacuuming
get out to the garden
wash the car

live

MY LIMIT

just don't ask me
to walk around Dublin
without you
I tried it yesterday
and had to grab a building
to stop myself falling
or spontaneously combusting
or crouching in a doorway
unable to participate in the hubbub
of Dublin streets
howling

SPEECHLESS

I could not speak
when I saw you
disintegrating
I had nothing to say
wordless
terror
each day
grasping
and holding you

SOCKS

I should know which month
to have the boiler serviced.
I'm scared.
Light bulbs keep
popping
and the house creaks
with scaredness
and all your beautiful
socks
are unmatched.

CHAOS THEORY

I grab my sides
I am disappearing
so I clutch my ribs
my arms
try to hold myself
together
I am dispersing
cells are abandoning ship

HELL

I cover my face.
Nothing to look at.
We did funny dances in the kitchen.
We sat on couches reading.
We went through hell.

Alien

You visited our planet
and tried
to blend in.
You did not blend in.
Our species
would ask –
who is that guy
in the jacket and tie?
You did your best with us
only
you landed
on this wrong impossible place:
poetry
is not oxygen
on our planet.
We hoped you
would stay here
amongst us
but you
could not breathe
here.

Abandoned

(after Cavafy)

Like the sound of a distant city –
the magnificent noise of our
life together – laughter, music, silence.
So stop cursing your happiness
that's disappeared,
plans in chaos, the world
a living hell – stop pointlessly moaning
about all of it.
As one long prepared for sadness
say goodbye to him:
your husband who is gone.
For heaven's sake, don't kid yourself
it was all a fairytale – it never happened.
Don't make a fool of yourself with hysterical scenarios.
As one long prepared for tragedy
(as is right for a poet's wife)
go bravely to the window
and listen for the last time
with sobs and courage
to the exquisite echo
of your time together
in this unknowable world
and say goodbye to him:
to the husband you have lost.

Me & Our House

I

just two sad-sacks
moping for you

not one of these
PhDs or Popes or Astrophysics experts

can solve the problem
of me & our house

moping for you

II

I'm in it right now
can the satellite of you
detect
the sonic boom
of me
wailing?

I'm transmitting
emergency radio waves
to whatever dark matter
you are now
sailing along
in your ship of death.

I had a house in Ireland
I had a life
I had a grocery list.
Do you see me?
Star I'm gazing at:
blink once for yes.

Dreams

You know that thing
where Yeats says
be careful where you're
treading
because you're clomping
around on my dreams?

I'd hate to show you
my dreams
right now.
They're trampled
into the mud
flat as a pancake.

What was it
we used to dream about?
All I sleep through
are nightmares.
It's dream-a-geddon.

Vow

No conversations
take place anymore
in our abode.
No rousing
Right!
when 6 a.m. arrives.

I hear no one
calling me
to come downstairs
for Sunday lunch,
Nobody welcomes me
when I open the door.

It's a chat-free zone.
I don't speak.
I must have made a
vow of silence.
I must be
a monk.

Dictation

I accept
that my eyes
and ears
no longer make sense
in our situation.
They are irrelevant.
Now I listen
with my cardiac area
and see
with my memory neurons.
Messenger
tell me how
it is with you.
I hold your pen
waiting for
dictation.

Here

I've crash-landed on a planet
covered with wall-to-wall people.
We had our own planet.
I don't have a map
for here.
Maybe it's a swamp
or a desert
or I've been eaten
by a sinkhole.
We heard tell of here.
We used to discuss
this place sometimes
but we were
never tempted
to visit.

Pup

I never thought
it would come
to this:
talking to a puppy
day in – day out.

She's a water-rescue breed
with webbed feet.
I bought her
to save me
from drowning.
But I'm drowning regardless.
The wind roars
down my chimney
and the tsunami starts.
My head sinks under the tide
but my water rescue puppy

looks over at me with sad eyes.

Pygmalion

You sculpted me
into shapes
year after year.
But I'm not a fan
of your new work.
I hate the new me
you've created.
I have no desire to be
Miss Pathetic
Miss Pat-on-the-Shoulder
Miss Was-the-Wife-of
Miss Widow-Woman.
It's not the image I was going for.

Ultimate Skellig

You can't even begin to imagine
how many craggy steps
need to be climbed
to get to my beehive hut.

You might possibly
make the mistake
of looking up
that's not a great idea
you could get dizzy
doing that.

Maybe you'll feel
like a sitdown and an aspirin half-way up
with a gale howling in your ear.

But then again
if the wind is strong enough
and ocean spit blasts your face
you might be in for a
journey to the very top
which you never expected.

Your foot might encounter
a slippery stone
and you could possibly
be guided by a host of angels
to a glorious eternity.

which was always the ultimate destination
of this Holy Place.

Hidden Words

You'd laugh at me
at the kitchen table
playing with my
'Circle a Word Jumbo'
puzzle booklet.
I sit for hours
searching for
hidden words.
I might as well.
The hidden word
for you
for what the hell is happening:
I can't find it
anywhere.

Faith

Walking in my Garden of Gethsemane
I come upon
an Angel of the Lord
Who sayeth unto me:
Dost thou think the Lord
hath forsaken thee?
Dost thou have such
rotten faith in his Goodness?
I sayeth unto this Angel:
What the hell am I supposed
to think?
Damnation! My one true friend
Hath been taken away from me
– see how YOU'D like it!
Now I sit alone – lost to the world.
What doth The Lord
have to say about THAT?

But the Angel of the Lord
shakes its head and sayeth:
Get over yourself.

Cyber You

I need to see you
living and breathing
– I go to YouTube
and there you are being you
(the tiny you)
with the tie I bought you
for Christmas.
Sitting on a chair
on a stage in Santa Fe
asking Seamus questions.
Eternally.

You in Mid-air

you in the yew tree
perched on a yew branch
over Lord Mayo's crypt
looking in this direction

or hovering like a drone
over my head
reminding me to do
household chores

don't fly off
I can feel how it is
with you
how light

you in mid-air
like mythological Sweeney
zooming around the foliage
of ancient Ireland

I see you
in the branches
staring this way
here's an orange

It'll Be OK

We all knew this day would come.
That it would be wet and misty since it's January
on this island – we all know about January – right?
So here it is.
The day your life's work heads off into the world.
Everything you saved –
every small ornate invitation and scribbled note.
Each word meticulously recorded and boxed.

FEDEX will be here soon.
The boxes stand quietly in the hallway
like little kids wearing hats and scarves
waiting nervously to go somewhere
they aren't that thrilled about.
I tell them it'll be OK.

Vinegar

Goddammit –
mopping the hallway
I drop the mop
And cover my ears –
this is the last straw:
Strauss's *Four Last Songs*
slaps me in the face
as I'm cleaning the floor
with vinegar and tears
such beautiful tiles in patterns
now just a blurry blob
under my feet
damp and disgusting

Our Cliff

I stand
at the edge of our cliff.
Gales are blowing –
I wonder
if I will be blown
over the precipice
to join you.

Maybe it won't be today.
I walk off
into the drizzle
and glance back
at the rectangle of earth
I'll sleep in with you
someday

Aghadoe

When I arrived in Aghadoe
in the Glen of the Birds
I found the softest moss
and lay down
with my cheek
resting on green
to wait for Dennis.
I would stay in this place
listening
for the sound
of his voice.

After Dennis O'Driscoll

I had everything:
a cozy house
a genius husband
a happy life
a Sunday roast
a flower garden with gravel paths

and then one day...